I'm On My Way Home Headed Up The Mountain

36 OF 700

BOOKS SPEAK FOR YOU

ACKNOWLEDGEMENT

I Would Like To Acknowledge The
CREATOR OF HEAVEN AND EARTH
(GOD) FOR ALL THAT HE HAS Given
Me. Thanking God I Am
For My Talents and Gifts.
I Recognize That The Lord Gave Me
This Gift, Which Allows Me To Share
With Children And Everyone That
Participates In The Reading Of The
Literary Material That I Produce
Through The Commission Of God.

Thank You
Lord God

I Will Forever Be Grateful
For Your Trust In Me
Pamela Denise Brown

To All Children

Loving You All

I Am.

Inspiring You To Love

God

As He Loves You

Through The

Inspiration

Of My Books.

WORDS
ARE
POWERFUL

Pamela Denise Brown
Goodwill Ambassador
For The Positive
Cultivation
Of Children
Author
Publisher
Illustrator
Editor

Books Speak For You books may be ordered
through Amazon, Createspace, booksellers or by
contacting:
Books Speak For You At
Booksspeakforyou.com
OR
Booksspeakforyou@yahoo.com
The views expressed in this work are solely those
of the author.
Any illustration provided by iStock and such
images are being used for illustrative purposes.
Certain stock imagery © iStock.
ISBN: 978-1-64050-037-2
Library of Congress Control Number:2017907773
Printed in the United States Of America

A Little Information About The Author

My Christian Books Are Designed To Encourage, Enlighten, Strengthen And Cause Children To Have A Closer Relationship With God And To Also Understand The Power Of Words.

I Create Christian Smart Books For Kids To Inspire, Illuminate, Brief, Encourage, Educate, Strengthen, Empower, Uplift, Enlighten, Equip, Develop, Cultivate, Notify, Advise, Update, Inform, Convert, Edify, Guide, Disclose AND Make Known The POWER Of God.

I Also Write Books To Educate Children, To Transform The Way A Child Thinks, To Better Children So They Can Become Successful People. I Write Books To Help Children Develop And Grow Psychologically.

As An Ambassador For The Cultivation Of Children, I Am A Trusted Source Moving To Inspire Children With Innovative Ideas, Creating Evolutionary Advancements By Urging Children To Open Up To New Ways Of Thinking In How They Deal With Others And Differences.

I Present Children With An Opportunity To Replicate And Scale The Ideas From The Pages Of The Encouraging Literature I Produce, Thereby Shaping The Lives Of Children From Any Background, Community, Age, Ethnicity Or gender.

I Dedicate
This Book
And
All Of My Children's
Books
To My Children
Carrayah, Gabriel &
Carrynn
AND
Every Child
Around The World

It Is With A Clear Understanding
That We Observe Jesus As The
Prince Of Peace In Our Own
Hearts,

So That Our Children Will Revere
Christ
As The Prince Of Peace In Theirs.
Jesus
A Guaranteed Source Of
Protection.
1:21 a.m. 7/5/2016

I'm

On

My

Way

Home

Headed
Up
The
Mountain

Rolling

Passing

The

Trees

Through

The

Valley

Alongside The Shore Strait To The Top

Passing

By

The

Sea

Everybody

Looking

Staring

At

Me

I Won't

Look

Back

There's

Nothing

Behind

Me

Everything

I

Need

To See

Is In

Front Of

Me

The

Tides

Are

High

The Race

Is

Sure

I'm On My Way

Home

Headed

Up The

Mountain

To An

Open Door

Everything

I

Do

Depends

On

Me

Jesus

Gave

His Life

And

Now

I'm

Free

Free

To

Love

Free

To

Give

Free

To

Understand

Why

I

Live

I'm

Headed

Up

The

Mountain

On My Way

Home

Rolling

Passing

The

Trees

Through

The

Valley

Alongside

The

Shore

Strait

To

The Top

Passing

By

The

Sea

Everybody

Looking

And

Staring

At

Me

I
Won't
Look
Back

There's Nothing Behind Me

Everything

I

Need

To

See

Is

In

Front

Of Me

The

Tides

Are

High

The

Race Is Sure

I'm

On

My

Way

Home

Headed

Up The

Mountain

To

An

Open

Door

CHILDREN
Do A Favor For Me
Write Your Own Rhyme About Going Up The Mountain To An Open Door And What That Means To You

_____
_____
_____
_____
_____
_____
_____
_____
_____
_____
_____
_____
_____
_____
_____
_____
_____
_____
_____
_____

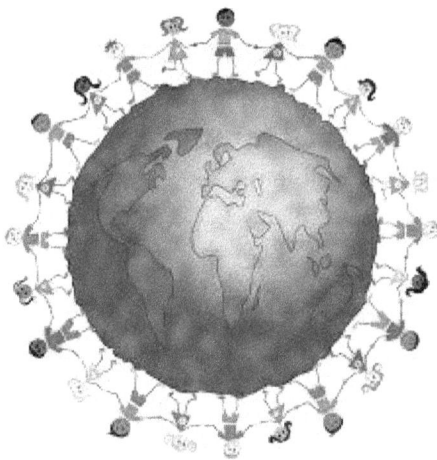

A Special

Dedication To
ALL THE CHILDREN WITH LOVE
IN COUNTRIES AROUND
THE WORLD

- A
- Afghanistan
- Albania
- Algeria
- Andorra
- Angola
- Antigua and Barbuda
- Argentina
- Armenia
- Australia
- Austria
- Azerbaijan
- B
- Bahamas
- Bahrain
- Bangladesh

- Barbados
- Belarus
- Belgium
- Belize
- Benin
- Bhutan
- Bolivia
- Bosnia and Herzegovina
- Botswana
- Brazil
- Brunei
- Bulgaria
- Burkina Faso
- Burundi
- C
- Cabo Verde
- Cambodia
- Cameroon
- Canada
- Central African Republic (CAR)
- Chad
- Chile
- China
- Colombia
- Comoros
- Democratic Republic of the Congo
- Republic of the Congo
- Costa Rica
- Cote d'Ivoire
- Croatia
- Cuba
- Cyprus
- Czech Republic
- D
- Denmark
- Djibouti
- Dominica
- Dominican Republic
- E
- Ecuador
- Egypt
- El Salvador
- Equatorial Guinea
- Eritrea
- Estonia

- Ethiopia
- F
- Fiji
- Finland
- France
- G
- Gabon
- Gambia
- Georgia
- Germany
- Ghana
- Greece
- Grenada
- Guatemala
- Guinea
- Guinea-Bissau
- Guyana

- H
- Haiti
- Honduras
- Hungary
- I
- Iceland
- India
- Indonesia
- Iran
- Iraq
- Ireland
- Israel
- Italy
- J
- Jamaica
- Japan
- Jordan
- K
- Kazakhstan
- Kenya
- Kiribati
- Kosovo
- Kuwait
- Kyrgyzstan
- L
- Laos
- Latvia
- Lebanon
- Lesotho
- Liberia
- Libya
- Liechtenstein
- Lithuania
- Luxembourg
- M

- Macedonia
- Madagascar
- Malawi
- Malaysia
- Maldives
- Mali
- Malta
- Marshall Islands
- Mauritania
- Mauritius
- Mexico
- Micronesia
- Moldova
- Monaco
- Mongolia
- Montenegro
- Morocco
- Mozambique
- Myanmar (Burma)
- N
- Namibia
- Nauru
- Nepal
- Netherlands
- New Zealand
- Nicaragua
- Niger
- Nigeria
- North Korea
- Norway
- O
- Oman
- P
- Pakistan
- Palau
- Palestine
- Panama
- Papua New Guinea
- Paraguay
- Peru
- Philippines
- Poland
- Portugal
- Q
- Qatar
- R
- Romania
- Russia
- Rwanda

- S
- St. Kitts and Nevis
- St. Lucia
- St. Vincent and the Grenadines
- Samoa
- San Marino
- Sao Tome and Principe
- Saudi Arabia
- Senegal
- Serbia
- Seychelles
- Sierra Leone
- Singapore
- Slovakia
- Slovenia
- Solomon Islands
- Somalia
- South Africa
- South Korea
- South Sudan
- Spain
- Sri Lanka
- Sudan
- Suriname
- Swaziland
- Sweden
- Switzerland
- Syria
- T
- Taiwan
- Tajikistan
- Tanzania
- Thailand
- Timor-Leste
- Togo
- Tonga
- Trinidad and Tobago
- Tunisia
- Turkey
- Turkmenistan
- Tuvalu
- U
- Uganda
- Ukraine
- United Arab Emirates (UAE)

- United Kingdom (UK)
- United States of America (USA)
- Uruguay
- Uzbekistan
- V
- Vanuatu
- Vatican City (Holy See)
- Venezuela
- Vietnam
- Y
- Yemen
- Z
- Zambia
- Zimbabwe

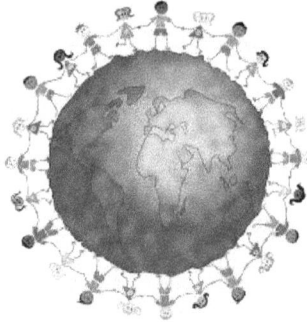

ANOTHER SPECIAL DEDICATION TO ALL THE CHILDREN WITH LOVE IN CITIES IN THE UNITED STATES OF AMERICA

Albany, NY
Albuquerque, NM
Anchorage, AK
Annapolis, MD
Atlanta, GA
Atlantic City, NJ
Augusta, ME
Austin, TX
Bakersfield, CA

Baltimore, MD
Baton Rouge, LA
Billings, MT
Biloxi, MS
Bismarck, ND
Bloomsburg, PA
Boise, ID
Boston, MA
Buffalo, NY
Burlington, VT
Carson City, NV

Charleston, SC
Charleston, WV
Charlotte, NC
Charlottesville, VA
Cheyenne, WY
Chicago, IL
Chicago, IL
Cleveland, OH
Colorado Springs, CO
Columbia, SC
Columbus, OH
Concord, CA
Concord, NH
Corpus Christi, TX
Dallas, TX
Davenport, IA
Daytona, FL
Denver, CO
Des Moines, IA
Des Plaines, IL
Detroit, MI
Dover, DE
Durham, NC
Erie, PA
Eugene, OR
Fayetteville, NC

Flagstaff, AZ
Frankfort, KY
Ft. Lauderdale, FL
Gettysburg, PA
Greenville, SC
Hampton Roads, VA
Harrisburg, PA
Hartford, CT
Helena, MT
Hollywood, CA
Honolulu, HI
Houston, TX
Huntsville, AL
Indianapolis, IN
Jackson, MS
Jackson Hole-Grand
Tetons, WY
Jacksonville, FL
Jefferson City, MO
Jim Thorpe, PA
Juneau, AK
Kansas City, MO
Knoxville, TN
Lake Tahoe, NV
Lancaster, PA

Lancaster / Central PA
Lansing, MI
Las Vegas, NV
Las Vegas, NV
Lexington, KY
Lincoln, NE
Little Rock, AR
Long Island, NY
Los Angeles, CA
Los Angeles, CA
Louisville, KY
Madison, WI
Manchester, NH
Maryville, TN
Memphis, TN
Miami, FL
Miami, FL
Milwaukee, WI
Minneapolis, MN
Mobile, AL
Montgomery, AL
Montpelier, VT
Morrison, IL
Nashville, TN
New Haven, CT

New Orleans, LA
New York: Bronx
New York: Brooklyn
New York: Manhattan
New York: Queens
New York City
Newark, NJ
Niagara Falls, NY
Northville, MI
Oklahoma City, OK
Orlando, FL
Olympia, WA
Omaha, NE
Orange County, CA
Palm Springs, CA
Pensacola, FL
Philadelphia, PA
Phoenix, AZ
Pierre, SD
Pittsburgh, PA
Portland, ME
Portland, OR
Providence, RI
Pueblo, CO
Raleigh, NC

Rapid City, SD
Reno, NV
Richmond, VA
Sacramento, CA
Salt Lake City, UT
San Diego, CA
San Francisco, CA
Santa Cruz, CA
Santa Fe, NM
Scranton, PA
Seattle, WA
Sedona, AZ
Shreveport, LA
Silicon Valley, CA
Springfield, IL
St. Joseph, MO
St. Paul, MN
St. Louis, MO

State College, PA
SurfScranton, PA
Syracuse, NY
Tacoma, WA
Tallahassee, FL
Tampa, FL
Topeka, KS
Trenton, NJ
Tulsa, OK
Tuscon, AZ
Tyler, TX
Washington, DC
Wichita, KS
Wilkes-Barre, PA
Williamsburg, VA
Williamsport, PA
Wilmington, DE
Yuma, AZ

It Is With A Clear Understanding
That We Observe Jesus As The
Prince Of Peace In Our Own
Hearts,

So That Our Children Will Revere
Christ
As The Prince Of Peace In Theirs.
Jesus
A Guaranteed Source Of
Protection.
1:21 a.m. 7/5/2016

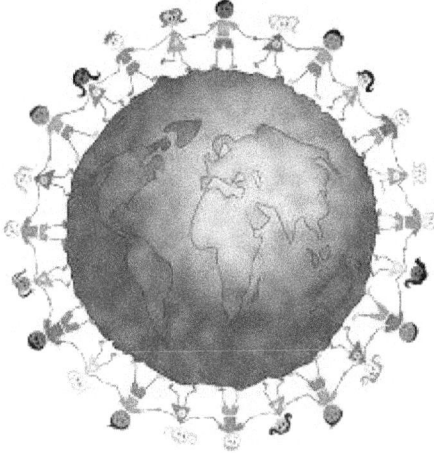

A Special

Dedication To
ALL THE CHILDREN WITH LOVE
IN COUNTRIES AROUND
THE WORLD

- A
- Afghanistan
- Albania
- Algeria
- Andorra
- Angola
- Antigua and Barbuda
- Argentina
- Armenia
- Australia
- Austria
- Azerbaijan
- B
- Bahamas
- Bahrain
- Bangladesh

- Barbados
- Belarus
- Belgium
- Belize
- Benin
- Bhutan
- Bolivia
- Bosnia and Herzegovina
- Botswana
- Brazil
- Brunei
- Bulgaria
- Burkina Faso
- Burundi
- C
- Cabo Verde
- Cambodia
- Cameroon
- Canada
- Central African Republic (CAR)
- Chad
- Chile
- China
- Colombia
- Comoros
- Democratic Republic of the Congo
- Republic of the Congo
- Costa Rica
- Cote d'Ivoire
- Croatia
- Cuba
- Cyprus
- Czech Republic
- D
- Denmark
- Djibouti
- Dominica
- Dominican Republic
- E
- Ecuador
- Egypt
- El Salvador
- Equatorial Guinea
- Eritrea
- Estonia

- Ethiopia
- F
- Fiji
- Finland
- France
- G
- Gabon
- Gambia
- Georgia
- Germany
- Ghana
- Greece
- Grenada
- Guatemala
- Guinea
- Guinea-Bissau
- Guyana

- H
- Haiti
- Honduras
- Hungary
- I
- Iceland
- India
- Indonesia
- Iran
- Iraq
- Ireland
- Israel
- Italy
- J
- Jamaica
- Japan
- Jordan
- K
- Kazakhstan
- Kenya
- Kiribati
- Kosovo
- Kuwait
- Kyrgyzstan
- L
- Laos
- Latvia
- Lebanon
- Lesotho
- Liberia
- Libya
- Liechtenstein
- Lithuania
- Luxembourg
- M

- Macedonia
- Madagascar
- Malawi
- Malaysia
- Maldives
- Mali
- Malta
- Marshall Islands
- Mauritania
- Mauritius
- Mexico
- Micronesia
- Moldova
- Monaco
- Mongolia
- Montenegro
- Morocco
- Mozambique
- Myanmar (Burma)
- N
- Namibia
- Nauru
- Nepal
- Netherlands
- New Zealand
- Nicaragua
- Niger
- Nigeria
- North Korea
- Norway
- O
- Oman
- P
- Pakistan
- Palau
- Palestine
- Panama
- Papua New Guinea
- Paraguay
- Peru
- Philippines
- Poland
- Portugal

- Q
- Qatar
- R
- Romania
- Russia
- Rwanda

- S
- St. Kitts and Nevis
- St. Lucia
- St. Vincent and the Grenadines
- Samoa
- San Marino
- Sao Tome and Principe
- Saudi Arabia
- Senegal
- Serbia
- Seychelles
- Sierra Leone
- Singapore
- Slovakia
- Slovenia
- Solomon Islands
- Somalia
- South Africa
- South Korea
- South Sudan
- Spain
- Sri Lanka
- Sudan
- Suriname
- Swaziland
- Sweden
- Switzerland
- Syria
- T
- Taiwan
- Tajikistan
- Tanzania
- Thailand
- Timor-Leste
- Togo
- Tonga
- Trinidad and Tobago
- Tunisia
- Turkey
- Turkmenistan
- Tuvalu
- U
- Uganda
- Ukraine
- United Arab Emirates (UAE)

- United Kingdom (UK)
- United States of America (USA)
- Uruguay
- Uzbekistan
- V
- Vanuatu
- Vatican City (Holy See)
- Venezuela
- Vietnam
- Y
- Yemen
- Z
- Zambia
- Zimbabwe

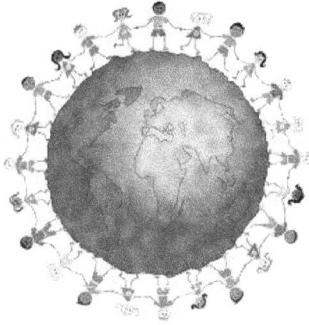

ANOTHER SPECIAL DEDICATION TO ALL THE CHILDREN WITH LOVE IN CITIES IN THE UNITED STATES OF AMERICA

Albany, NY
Albuquerque, NM
Anchorage, AK
Annapolis, MD
Atlanta, GA
Atlantic City, NJ
Augusta, ME
Austin, TX
Bakersfield, CA

Baltimore, MD
Baton Rouge, LA
Billings, MT
Biloxi, MS
Bismarck, ND
Bloomsburg, PA
Boise, ID
Boston, MA
Buffalo, NY

Burlington, VT
Carson City, NV
Charleston, SC
Charleston, WV
Charlotte, NC
Charlottesville, VA
Cheyenne, WY
Chicago, IL
Chicago, IL
Cleveland, OH
Colorado Springs, CO
Columbia, SC
Columbus, OH
Concord, CA
Concord, NH
Corpus Christi, TX
Dallas, TX
Davenport, IA
Daytona, FL
Denver, CO
Des Moines, IA
Des Plaines, IL
Detroit, MI
Dover, DE
Durham, NC
Erie, PA

Eugene, OR
Fayetteville, NC
Flagstaff, AZ
Frankfort, KY
Ft. Lauderdale, FL
Gettysburg, PA
Greenville, SC
Hampton Roads, VA
Harrisburg, PA
Hartford, CT
Helena, MT
Hollywood, CA
Honolulu, HI
Houston, TX
Huntsville, AL
Indianapolis, IN
Jackson, MS
Jackson Hole-Grand
Tetons, WY
Jacksonville, FL
Jefferson City, MO
Jim Thorpe, PA
Juneau, AK
Kansas City, MO
Knoxville, TN
Lake Tahoe, NV

Lancaster, PA
Lancaster / Central PA
Lansing, MI
Las Vegas, NV
Las Vegas, NV
Lexington, KY
Lincoln, NE
Little Rock, AR
Long Island, NY
Los Angeles, CA
Los Angeles, CA
Louisville, KY
Madison, WI
Manchester, NH
Maryville, TN
Memphis, TN
Miami, FL
Miami, FL
Milwaukee, WI
Minneapolis, MN
Mobile, AL
Montgomery, AL
Montpelier, VT
Morrison, IL
Nashville, TN

New Haven, CT
New Orleans, LA
New York: Bronx
New York: Brooklyn
New York: Manhattan
New York: Queens
New York City
Newark, NJ
Niagara Falls, NY
Northville, MI
Oklahoma City, OK
Orlando, FL
Olympia, WA
Omaha, NE
Orange County, CA
Palm Springs, CA
Pensacola, FL
Philadelphia, PA
Phoenix, AZ
Pierre, SD
Pittsburgh, PA
Portland, ME
Portland, OR
Providence, RI
Pueblo, CO

Raleigh, NC
Rapid City, SD
Reno, NV
Richmond, VA
Sacramento, CA
Salt Lake City, UT
San Diego, CA
San Francisco, CA
Santa Cruz, CA
Santa Fe, NM
Scranton, PA
Seattle, WA
Sedona, AZ
Shreveport, LA
Silicon Valley, CA
Springfield, IL
St. Joseph, MO
St. Paul, MN
St. Louis, MO
State College, PA
SurfScranton, PA
Syracuse, NY
Tacoma, WA
Tallahassee, FL
Tampa, FL
Topeka, KS

Trenton, NJ
Tulsa, OK
Tuscon, AZ
Tyler, TX
Washington, DC
Wichita, KS
Wilkes-Barre, PA
Williamsburg, VA
Williamsport, PA
Wilmington, DE
Yuma, AZ

THE BOOKS
700 BOOKS IN 60 DAYS

I was commissioned by God to first write 40 books in 40 days, which I completed June 2015, Then commissioned again by God to write
100 books in 100 days
On October 1, 2015, which I completed
January 8, 2016.
Commissioned Again June 7, 2016 to write 700 books in 60 days starting in July, 2016,
IF YOU ARE READING THIS IT MEANS I COMPLETED THEM

Thank You

For Purchasing This Book. In Your Purchase, You Are Celebrating With Me, The Completion Of One Of God's Many Works Through Me.

This Book Represents, The Completion Of Writing 700 Children's Books In 60 Days. 100 Of Which, Are Written In 5 Different Languages

Contact Information

Publisher: Books Speak For You
Website: Booksspeakforyou.com
1-800-757-0598
Email: Booksspeakforyou@yahoo.com

To Schedule School Visits Or Learning
Centers By Author For Cup Cakes And
Conversations, Contact
Author: Pamela Denise Brown
267-318-8933

www.ingramcontent.com/pod-product-compliance
Lightning Source LLC
Chambersburg PA
CBHW071733020426
42331CB00008B/2011